Tennessee

by Fran Hodgkins

Consultant:
Dr. Thomas E. Bibler
Emeritus Professor
University of Tennessee at Chattanooga
Tennessee Council for the Social Studies

Capstone *press*
Mankato, Minnesota

Capstone Press
151 Good Counsel Drive • P.O. Box 669 • Mankato, Minnesota 56002
http://www.capstone-press.com

Library of Congress Cataloging-in-Publication Data
Hodgkins, Fran, 1964–
 Tennessee / by Fran Hodgkins.
 v. cm.—(Land of liberty)
 Includes bibliographical references (p. 61) and index.
 Contents: About Tennessee—The land, climate, and wildlife—The history of Tennessee—Government and politics—Economy and resources—People and culture—Recipe—Almanac—Timeline—Words to know.
 ISBN 0-7368-2199-6 (hardcover)
 1. Tennessee—Juvenile literature. [1. Tennessee.] I. Title. II. Series.
F436.3.H63 2004
976.8—dc21   2002154704

Summary: An introduction to the geography, history, government, politics, economy, resources, people, and culture of Tennessee, including maps, charts, and a recipe.

Editorial Credits

Carrie Braulick, editor; Jennifer Schonborn, series designer; Linda Clavel, book designer; Enoch Peterson, illustrator; Jo Miller, photo researcher; Eric Kudalis, product planning editor

Photo Credits

Cover images: Memphis, Visuals Unlimited/Scott Berner; Great Smoky Mountains, Pat and Chuck Blackley

Capstone Press/Gary Sundermeyer, 54; Corbis, 29; Corbis/Bettmann, 30, 50; Corbis/Raymond Gehman, 12–13, 16–17; Digital Stock, 56; Folio Inc./Marilyn Davids, 52–53; Gary Braasch, 8; Getty Images/Stock Montage/Archive Photos, 36; Getty Images/Mario Tama, 63; Houserstock/Dave G. Houser, 4, 32, 40, 42; Mira.com/ Ron Sherman, 38; North Wind Picture Archives, 18, 22; One Mile Up, Inc., 55 (both); PhotoDisc Inc., 1; Stock Montage Inc., 21, 24, 26, 58; The Viesti Collection Inc./Joe Viesti, 46; Unicorn Stock Photos/Robert W. Ginn, 43; U.S. Postal Service, 59; Visuals Unlimited/Ken Lucas, 14; Visuals Unlimited/Jeff Greenberg, 51; Visuals Unlimited/Gary W. Carter, 57; Wolfgang Kaehler/ www.wkaehlerphoto.com, 44–45

Artistic Effects

Corbis, PhotoDisc Inc.

1 2 3 4 5 6 08 07 06 05 04 03

Table of Contents

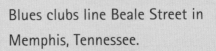

Blues clubs line Beale Street in Memphis, Tennessee.

Chapter 1

About Tennessee

For many blues music lovers, Beale Street in Memphis, Tennessee, is a favorite street. W. C. Handy wrote many of the first successful blues songs in clubs along Beale Street. Blues music, which developed from African spiritual music, became popular in the early 1900s. It often consisted of guitar and piano music. During the 1920s, many blues performers came to Beale Street clubs to entertain audiences.

Today, Beale Street is a popular tourist attraction. Many blues musical events take place at Handy Park. The Blues Foundation is located in Handy's former

Did you know…?
Eight states border
Tennessee. Only Missouri
has as many neighbors as
Tennessee does.

house on Beale Street. This
organization promotes blues
music throughout the world.

The Volunteer State

One of Tennessee's nicknames is the Volunteer State.
Tennesseans who volunteered to fight in the War
of 1812 (1812–1814) earned the state its nickname.
Tennesseans have continued their willingness to fight
in other wars. During the Civil War (1861–1865),
Tennessee sent more soldiers to battle than any
other state.

Tennessee is also known as the Big Bend State.
The Tennessee River flows beyond the state's southern
border into Alabama and then back again. It creates a
gigantic U-shaped bend.

Tennessee is a southeastern state. The long, thin
state borders many other states. To the north of
Tennessee are Kentucky and Virginia. North Carolina

Tennessee Cities

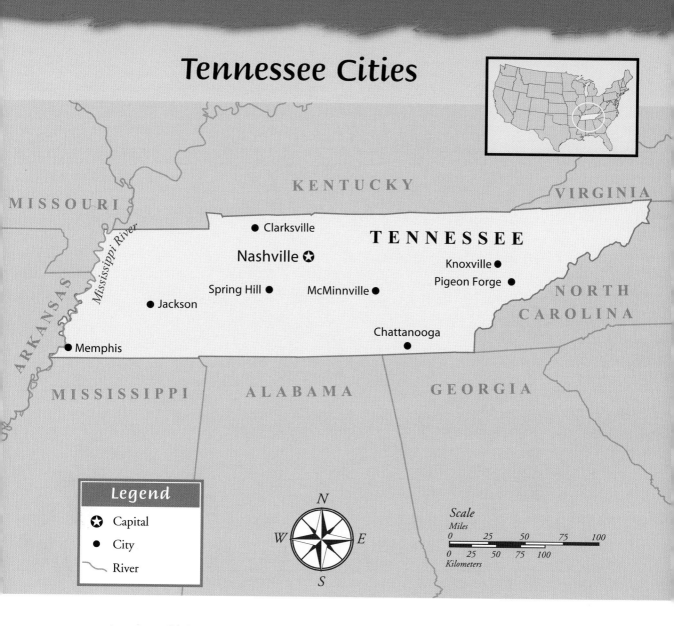

is east of Tennessee. To the south, Tennessee shares a border with Georgia, Alabama, and Mississippi. Tennessee's neighbors to the west are Arkansas and Missouri.

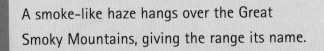
A smoke-like haze hangs over the Great
Smoky Mountains, giving the range its name.

Chapter 2

Land, Climate, and Wildlife

Tennessee has mountains, valleys, and streams. Much of the state is covered with forests. Because of its varied land, many people say that Tennessee is like three states in one. The state divides naturally into three land regions. These regions are East Tennessee, Middle Tennessee, and West Tennessee.

East Tennessee

East Tennessee is mountainous and covered with forests. The Unaka, Great Smoky, and Cumberland Mountains lie in this region. These ranges are part of a larger mountain range called

the Appalachians. The Appalachian Mountains run from Georgia northeast to Canada.

Great Smoky Mountains National Park is part of East Tennessee. The park attracts thousands of visitors every year. Clingmans Dome, Tennessee's highest point, is in the park. This mountain peak rises 6,643 feet (2,025 meters) above sea level.

The Great Valley lies west of Great Smoky Mountains National Park. It runs from Alabama north to New York. Many Tennessee farmers raise crops in the valley's fertile land.

Middle Tennessee

The Central Basin makes up Middle Tennessee. This flat, low region is oval-shaped. It is bordered by mountains to the east and rolling hills to the west. The Tennessee River encircles the basin. The Central Basin includes some of Tennessee's most fertile land. Farmers grow crops and let their livestock graze in the area.

Tennessee's Land Features

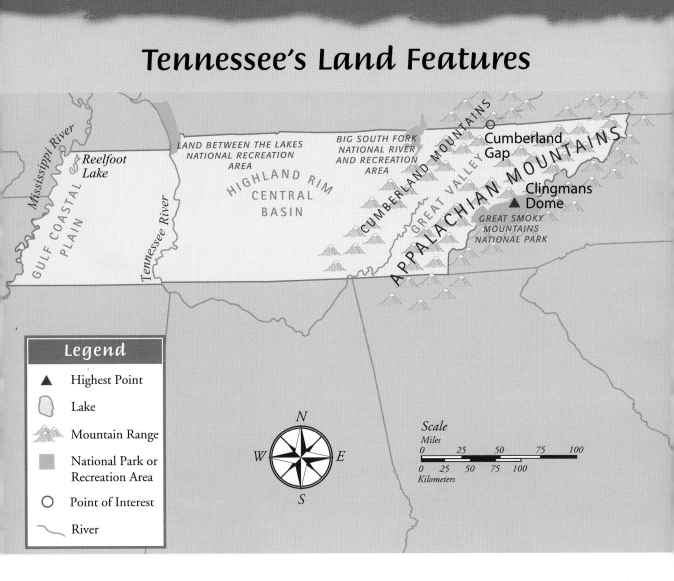

Legend

▲ Highest Point
🝆 Lake
⛰ Mountain Range
▨ National Park or Recreation Area
○ Point of Interest
〜 River

Mississippi River

Reelfoot Lake

GULF COASTAL PLAIN

Tennessee River

LAND BETWEEN THE LAKES NATIONAL RECREATION AREA

HIGHLAND RIM CENTRAL BASIN

BIG SOUTH FORK NATIONAL RIVER AND RECREATION AREA

CUMBERLAND MOUNTAINS

GREAT VALLEY

APPALACHIAN MOUNTAINS

Cumberland Gap

Clingmans Dome

GREAT SMOKY MOUNTAINS NATIONAL PARK

N W E S

Scale

Miles
0   25   50   75   100

0   25   50   75   100
Kilometers

The Highland Rim surrounds the Central Basin. Farmers grow tobacco and cotton in the Highland Rim. Limestone, iron, and other minerals are mined in this hilly area.

West Tennessee

West Tennessee is part of a large U.S. region called the Gulf Coastal Plain. The Gulf Coastal Plain extends from the Gulf of Mexico north to southern Illinois. Many low hills and streams make up the region.

The Mississippi River is at Tennessee's western border. Many of West Tennessee's smaller rivers empty into the Mississippi. A part of West Tennessee is known as the Delta. The Mississippi River makes the soil in the Delta perfect for growing crops.

Reelfoot Lake lies in the northwestern corner of Tennessee. It is the state's only natural lake. People have made the rest of the lakes in Tennessee. Before 1811, Reelfoot Lake did not exist. During the winter of 1811–1812, a series of large earthquakes struck Tennessee. Known as the New Madrid earthquakes, they caused a large area of land to drop several feet. Water from the nearby Mississippi River roared into the lowered land, creating the lake. Today, many people fish in the lake's shallow water. The area is home to the largest winter population of bald eagles in the eastern United States.

Bald cypress trees grow in the shallow waters of Reelfoot Lake.

The Red Wolf

In the past, the red wolf lived throughout the southern United States. But as people cleared forests to build, the red wolf became endangered. By 1970, only 100 red wolves remained. These wolves lived in a small patch of land in Louisiana and Texas.

Since the 1980s, people have been working to increase the red wolf's range. In 1991, red wolves were reintroduced to Great Smoky Mountains National Park. They began to reproduce. By 1993, the red wolf population in the park had grown to 16 animals. Today, about 40 red wolves live in the park.

Climate

Tennessee's climate is mild. In summer, the temperature averages 76 degrees Fahrenheit (24 degrees Celsius). Winters have an average temperature of 39 degrees Fahrenheit (4 degrees Celsius). Temperatures vary according to the land regions. The warmest temperatures are in West Tennessee. The coldest temperatures are in the mountains of East Tennessee.

Total precipitation in Tennessee averages 52 inches (132 centimeters) a year. Most of the state's precipitation is rain. The mild temperatures make snow rare. Large amounts of rain can cause Tennessee's major rivers to flood. In March 2002, heavy rains and flooding killed seven people and destroyed hundreds of homes in Tennessee.

Plants and Wildlife

Tennessee's varied landscape supports different types of plants and wildlife. The state's woodlands are made up of hickory, oak, elm, pine, walnut, and tulip trees. Wildflowers are common in Tennessee. These include daisies, saxifrage, dragonroot, and yellow jasmine. Purple and pink blossoms of the hepatica grow during winter. Native grasses called little bluestem and big bluestem grow throughout the state. Shrubs include rhododendron and dogwood.

Many animals live in Tennessee's forests. These animals include black bears, deer, raccoons, foxes, bobcats, and rabbits. Many of these animals also make their homes in the farmland areas of the state. Herons and egrets nest near Tennessee's rivers. Trout, bass, and catfish swim in the rivers.

Tennessee has about 90 animals that are in danger of dying out. Among these endangered species are the royal snail, the Nashville crayfish, the lake sturgeon, and the eastern cougar. Some animals in Tennessee are considered threatened. These species may soon become endangered. They include the silverjaw minnow, the Tennessee cave salamander, the golden eagle, and the river otter.

Caves

Tennessee has more than 8,000 caves. Many more caves may still be undiscovered. In the city of Sweetwater, cave visitors can ride in a glass-bottomed boat to explore a lake called the Lost Sea. This lake is the largest underground lake in the United States.

Cumberland Caverns, near McMinnville, is Tennessee's largest cave that is open to the public. Some people hold banquets, parties, and weddings in the cave.

Visitors to Cumberland Caverns see a variety of rock formations. Water seeping through cracks in limestone rock created the formations over thousands of years.

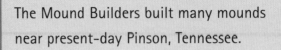

The Mound Builders built many mounds near present-day Pinson, Tennessee.

Chapter 3

History of Tennessee

Thousands of years ago, the Tennessee area had a thick covering of plants. Part of the land was underwater. Mammoths and other animals that have died out roamed the land. Today, scientists find fossils from these ancient animals in central and western Tennessee.

American Indians were the first people living in Tennessee. Before the 1500s, a group called the Mound Builders lived there. These Indians built large mounds out of the soil. By the 1600s, the major Indian nations in Tennessee were the Creek, Cherokee, Shawnee, and Chickasaw.

First Europeans

In the mid-1500s, the first Europeans arrived in Tennessee. In 1540, Spanish explorer Hernando de Soto arrived there seeking gold for Spain. De Soto and his soldiers believed the American Indians had hidden gold. They raided many Indian villages. Some of the Spanish soldiers were sick with diseases. The Indians had never been exposed to these European diseases. Thousands of American Indians became sick and died.

Europeans did not return to Tennessee until the late 1600s. In 1673, Englishmen Gabriel Arthur and James Needham came to Tennessee from North Carolina. They hoped to trade with the American Indians for animal furs. At the time, the fur trade was a growing business. Europeans used the furs to make hats and clothing.

Frenchmen Louis Jolliet and Jacques Marquette also came to Tennessee in 1673. Jolliet wanted to trade with the Indians for furs. Marquette was a missionary who wanted to teach Christianity to the Indians.

By the early 1700s, both Great Britain, which England had become a part of, and France wanted control of land in North

America. The two countries fought the French and Indian War (1754–1763). Great Britain won the war and claimed all land east of the Mississippi River. Great Britain already had 13 colonies on the east coast of North America.

In the Proclamation of 1763, King George III of Great Britain stated that the colonists could not settle the land west of the Appalachian Mountains. British rulers did not want the colonists so far away from their control.

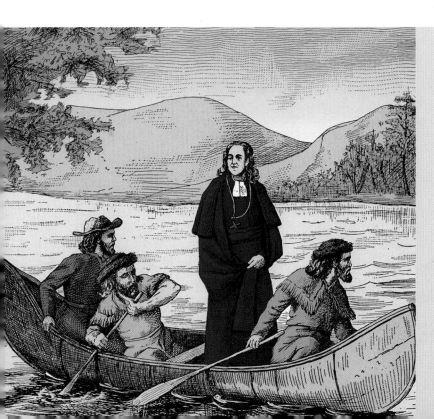

Missionary Jacques Marquette (standing) came to the Tennessee area in 1673.

Settlers traveled through the Cumberland Gap to reach the Tennessee area throughout the late 1700s and early 1800s.

Settlers in Tennessee

British colonists wanted to move west of the mountains because the colonies had become crowded. They ignored the Proclamation of 1763. By 1770, small groups of settlers from North Carolina, South Carolina, and Virginia had moved to eastern Tennessee.

In 1772, these colonists formed a government called the Watauga Association. The Watauga Association lasted until 1775. North Carolina began governing the area in 1776.

Many colonists had difficulty moving to the Tennessee region. The Appalachian and Cumberland Mountains were difficult to travel across. Early settlers passed through a natural break in the mountains called the Cumberland Gap. The Cumberland Gap is located where the modern-day borders of Kentucky, Tennessee, and Virginia meet.

In March 1775, Daniel Boone led a group of men to blaze a trail across the Appalachians. The trail went through the Cumberland Gap. The colonists then could travel more easily to the Tennessee region. The trail later became known as the Wilderness Road.

Revolutionary War and Statehood

In April, the Revolutionary War (1775–1783) started. The colonists fought against Britain for their independence. Settlers in Tennessee helped the colonies fight the British.

In 1780, some settlers learned that the British were planning to attack western settlements across the Appalachians. Tennessee settler John Sevier led a group of

After fierce fighting, the colonists won the Battle of Kings Mountain. The victory stopped the British from advancing into North Carolina.

men east across the mountains. There, they met and joined with colonists. Together, the men defeated a group of British soldiers on Kings Mountain in South Carolina. In 1783, the colonists won the Revolutionary War, and the United States became an independent country.

By the late 1700s, many settlers had traveled the Wilderness Road into the Tennessee area. In 1789, North Carolina gave up its claim to Tennessee. The federal government then gained control of it. The area became known as the Southwest Territory. The territory's population was soon large enough for it to become a state. On June 1, 1796, Tennessee became the 16th state. Sevier became Tennessee's first governor.

The Civil War

Throughout the early 1800s, Northern and Southern states had many disagreements. Northerners and Southerners argued about how much power state governments should have. Southern states, including Tennessee, forced African American slaves to work on large farms called plantations. People in the Northern states depended on manufacturing more than farming. Many Northerners believed slavery was wrong.

By 1861, the issues separating the North and South still were not resolved. The Civil War began after seven Southern states seceded from, or left, the United States. These states formed their own country called the Confederate States of America.

Tennessee was the last state to join the Confederacy. Many Tennessee soldiers disagreed with the decision. Many of the state's soldiers fought for the North, or the Union, instead of the Confederacy.

Near the end of the Civil War, U.S. President Abraham Lincoln was murdered. His vice president, Tennessean Andrew Johnson, became president. After the war, Tennessee became the first state to rejoin the Union.

Tennessee was the site of many Civil War battles, including the Battle of Fort Sanders near Knoxville.

Reconstruction

Reconstruction of the South started after the Civil War and continued for several years. The Civil War had destroyed much of Tennessee. Roads, farms, factories, and towns had to be rebuilt.

African Americans were free after the Civil War. But they struggled to live in Tennessee and other Southern states. Many African Americans moved from plantations to cities. Others rented a part of a plantation owner's farm. Most African Americans earned little money. They did not have equal rights with whites. In 1866, some white Tennesseans formed the Ku Klux Klan. Members of the group threatened and killed African Americans.

The Early and Mid-1900s

In 1917, the United States entered World War I (1914–1918). More than 100,000 Tennessee men volunteered for service. One of them was a man named Alvin York. York became one of the war's heroes. On October 8, 1918, York and a small group of men captured more than 100 enemy soldiers.

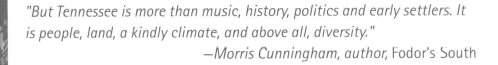
From 1929 to 1939, the United States suffered the Great Depression. Many people lost their jobs and homes. Federal and state governments started programs that gave people jobs. In Tennessee, people got work through the Tennessee Valley Authority (TVA) building dams and planting trees. The dams used water to provide electricity to the entire region. Some TVA workers developed fertilizers to help farmers' crops grow. Today, the TVA continues to supply electricity to thousands of Tennesseans.

World War II (1939–1945) helped bring the United States out of the Great Depression. People worked making airplanes, guns, and other supplies for the war. Some people did research at the Oak Ridge National Laboratory in Oak Ridge, Tennessee. These researchers studied atomic energy. They helped create two atomic bombs. The bombs were dropped on two Japanese cities in 1945. The destruction that these attacks caused helped bring the war to an end.

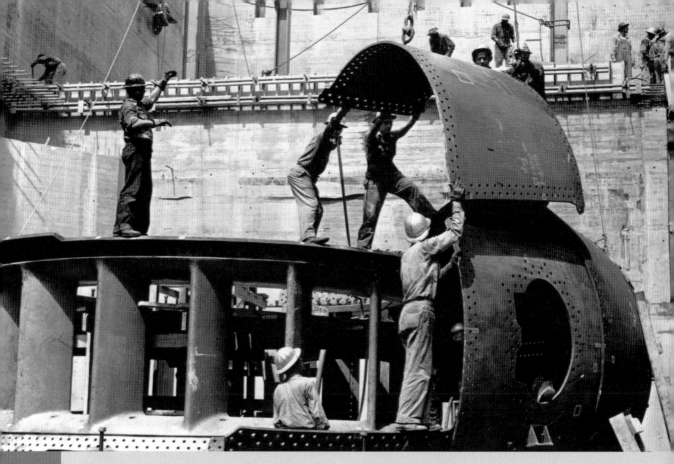
Many Tennesseans worked through the Tennessee Valley Authority building dams during the Great Depression.

Recent Times

African Americans in the South struggled to gain equal rights during the Civil Rights movement of the mid-1950s and 1960s. Until this time, African Americans were required to use facilities separate from white people. African Americans could not stay in the same hotels, attend the same public

Civil rights marches were common in the southern United States during the Civil Rights movement. U.S. National Guard troops often had to keep marches from becoming violent.

schools, or drink from the same water fountains as white people. These practices were known as segregation.

In the late 1950s, the state began to allow African Americans to attend the same schools as whites. The process was called integration. Nashville became the first major city in the south to begin integrating public places. In 1964, the U.S. Congress passed the Civil Rights Act. This law made all forms of discrimination illegal.

Since the 1980s, Tennessee has become prosperous. The Tombigbee Waterway opened in 1985. This waterway connects the Tennessee and Tombigbee Rivers. Ships that use the waterway can travel quickly from the southern United States to ports along the Gulf of Mexico. This waterway has helped Tennessee businesses trade goods with other countries. The state's tourism industry has strengthened in recent years. Tennessee's growing economy has attracted more businesses and people to the state. The population grew 16 percent from 1990 to 2000.

Many of Tennessee's government workers have offices at the state capitol building in Nashville.

Chapter 4

Government and Politics

Famous U.S. architect William Strickland was hired to design Nashville's capitol building in 1845. Strickland died in 1854 before the building was complete. To honor his work, his body was placed into a vault that was built within the capitol's northeast wall.

State Government

The state government in Tennessee includes the executive, legislative, and judicial branches. The executive branch carries out laws. The governor, who is elected to four-year terms, leads the executive branch. The branch also includes the lieutenant governor and other elected officials.

Government departments, boards, and commissions are part of the executive branch. Some of Tennessee's most important departments are the Department of Agriculture, Department of Transportation, Department of Corrections, and the Department of Education. Among the state's boards and commissions is the Tennessee Commission for Film, Entertainment, and Music. This group works to bring movie and music producers to the state.

The legislative branch is known as the General Assembly. This branch suggests and makes laws. The senate and the house of representatives make up the General Assembly. The senate has 33 members, and the house of representatives has 99 members. Senators serve four-year terms, and representatives serve two-year terms.

The judicial branch is made up of all the courts in the state. The supreme court is the highest of these courts. It

Tennessee's State Government

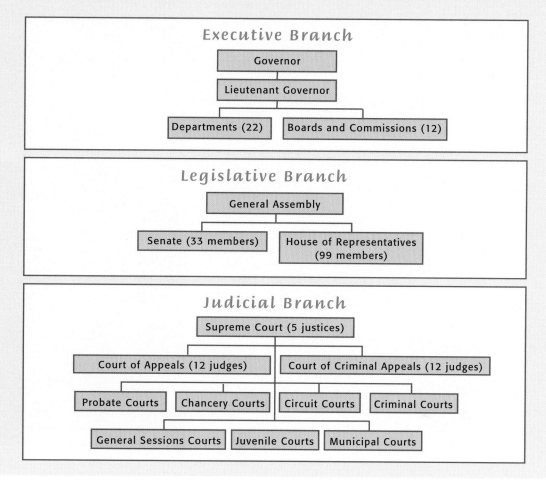

Executive Branch

Governor

Lieutenant Governor

Departments (22) | Boards and Commissions (12)

Legislative Branch

General Assembly

Senate (33 members) | House of Representatives (99 members)

Judicial Branch

Supreme Court (5 justices)

Court of Appeals (12 judges) | Court of Criminal Appeals (12 judges)

Probate Courts | Chancery Courts | Circuit Courts | Criminal Courts

General Sessions Courts | Juvenile Courts | Municipal Courts

is made up of a chief justice and four associate justices. The supreme court reviews cases on appeal and makes the final decision. The system of lower courts holds trials for criminals or deals with cases that have been appealed.

Andrew Johnson

Tennessean Andrew Johnson was U.S. president from 1865 to 1869. Johnson faced the difficult task of rebuilding the South after the Civil War. Before the war, he had been a U.S. senator. He disagreed with secession. When Johnson became president, he tried to bring the Southern states back into the Union. But some senators from Northern states thought Johnson should punish the Southern states for seceding.

These senators tried to remove Johnson from office by putting him on trial for misconduct. The House impeached Johnson. But a single vote in the Senate saved him from the dishonor, and Johnson finished his term.

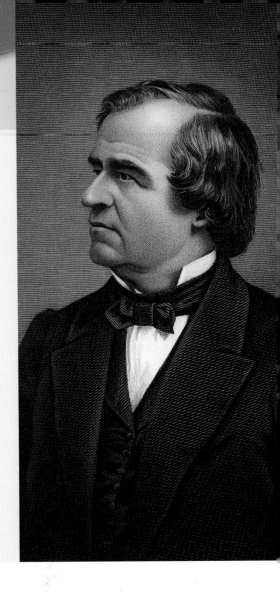

County and Local Government

Tennessee is made up of 95 counties. County governments are structured like state government, with an executive, legislative, and judicial branch.

Most cities and towns in Tennessee have the Mayor-Aldermanic Charter form of government. Voters elect a mayor and a Board of Aldermen. The mayor acts as the executive officer. The Board of Aldermen is the legislative body.

Tennessee Politics

Historically, Tennessee has voted for Democratic candidates. In the last several decades, the state has voted for mainly Republican presidential candidates.

Many Tennesseans have played a role in national politics. U.S. Presidents Andrew Jackson and Andrew Johnson lived in the state.

Democrat Al Gore was born in Washington, D.C., but he became a famous Tennessee politician. He worked as a reporter for *The Tennessean* newspaper in the early 1970s. He then went to law school at Vanderbilt University. He served in the U.S. House of Representatives from 1977 to 1985. In 1985, he became a U.S. senator from Tennessee. He then served as U.S. vice president from 1993 to 2001. Gore ran for president in 2000. He lost the election to Republican George W. Bush.

The Nissan Motor Manufacturing
Corporation is one of Tennessee's
largest employers.

Chapter 5

Economy and Resources

In the 1940s, Tennessee's mainly agricultural economy changed. Many people found work in factories. By the 1960s, Tennessee was mainly an industrial state. Today, most Tennesseans hold jobs in the manufacturing and service industries.

Manufacturing

Car manufacturing is one of Tennessee's most important industries. General Motors produces Saturn cars in Spring Hill. The Saturn plant has been making cars since 1990. It is one of the five largest employers in the state. Nissan Motor Manufacturing Corporation has a plant in Smyrna.

The Country Music Hall of Fame and Museum is a tourist attraction in Nashville.

Tennessee factories produce a wide variety of products. A top computer systems company, Dell, has manufacturing plants in Lebanon and Nashville. Other leading Tennessee manufacturers are Lockheed Martin, an aircraft company, and Eastman Chemical, which manufactures industrial chemicals. The state is also home to Jimmy Dean sausage products, Little Debbie snack cakes, Russell Stover Candies, and Jack Daniel's Distillery, makers of Tennessee whiskey.

Service Industries

Many companies in Tennessee provide services. Workers in service industries have jobs in many areas, including hotels, restaurants, government, banking, education, and health care. Federal Express, a worldwide shipping service, has its headquarters in Memphis. Columbia/HCA Healthcare Corporation is based in Nashville. It is the nation's largest chain of hospitals. Olan Mills, an international chain of photography studios, has its headquarters in Chattanooga.

Tourism is one of Tennessee's largest industries. Country music lovers come to Nashville where they visit the Grand Ole Opry and the Country Music Hall of Fame and Museum. The Grand Ole Opry is a concert hall and live radio show. It is the longest continually running radio show in the world.

The Peabody Hotel

Visitors to Memphis often go to the Peabody Hotel. The Peabody has ducks in its lobby from 11:00 in the morning to 5:00 in the afternoon each day. In the 1930s, the hotel's general manager thought it would be a great joke to put some live ducks into the fountain of the hotel lobby. The guests liked the ducks, and ducks have been residents ever since. The ducks live in a place built for them called the "Duck Palace" on the roof. Every day, the hotel's "duckmaster" leads them down in the elevator to the lobby fountain.

Rock music fans visit the Gibson guitar factory and the Memphis Rock 'n' Soul Museum in Memphis.

Tennessee is known for attractions besides music. Some people visit the former home of one of the most famous U.S. railroad engineers, Casey Jones. The home and a railroad museum are in Jackson. Tennessee's many state and national parks and recreational areas also draw thousands of visitors. Some tourists visit the world's largest freshwater aquarium in Chattanooga. In Pigeon Forge, more than 2.5 million people visit the Dollywood theme park each year.

Agriculture

In 1997, farmland made up about 43 percent of the total land in Tennessee. Tobacco and cotton are two of the state's most important crops. Tennessee farmers also grow corn, soybeans, wheat, vegetables, and fruit.

Tobacco is Tennessee's most valuable crop.

The state's top agricultural products include beef cattle, dairy products, and poultry, especially broiler chickens. Tennessee farmers also raise sheep, hogs, catfish, and trout. In 1997, livestock accounted for about 47 percent of all the agricultural income in the state.

Tennessee is also famous for its horses. Many people raise horses on large farms. The Tennessee Walking Horse was bred in Tennessee in the early 1900s. It is known throughout the world for its smooth ride.

Forestry

Forest products are an important part of the Tennessee economy. The state is one of the nation's leading producers of wood products from oak, walnut, and hickory. Together, the raw and processed farm and forestry products are the state's leading exports. They bring in more than $2.1 billion each year. Tennessee is also a leading provider of nursery stock. These plants are sold to gardeners and home owners.

Tennessee Walking Horses were first bred in Tennessee. Today, people raise them throughout the United States.

Tennessee holds several festivals each year, including the Fiddlers' Jamboree.

Chapter 6

People and Culture

Tennesseans celebrate their culture in several ways. Many of Tennessee's ethnic groups hold yearly festivals to celebrate their heritage. Tennesseans with German backgrounds celebrate Oktoberfest in Nashville's Germantown neighborhood. People of Scottish heritage hold highland games at various places around the state. Participants at these events compete in races and contests of strength and skill. American Indians come together at intertribal powwows. African Americans celebrate their heritage in many festivals, including the African American Street Festival in Nashville.

Tennesseans have many backgrounds. Most Tennesseans are white. They are descendants of people from Europe. Many Europeans came to Tennessee from Italy, Ireland, Scotland, and Germany. About 16 percent of Tennesseans are African Americans. Many African Americans live in or near Memphis in Shelby County. Compared to many other states, few Tennesseans are Asian, Hispanic, or American Indian.

About 60 percent of Tennesseans live in or near the state's largest cities. These cities include Memphis, Nashville, Knoxville, and Chattanooga.

Food

Tennessee is famous for Memphis barbecue ribs. Rather than being smothered in sauce, Memphis barbecue ribs are rubbed with spices and salt. They are cooked slowly over a fire.

Tennessee's Ethnic Backgrounds

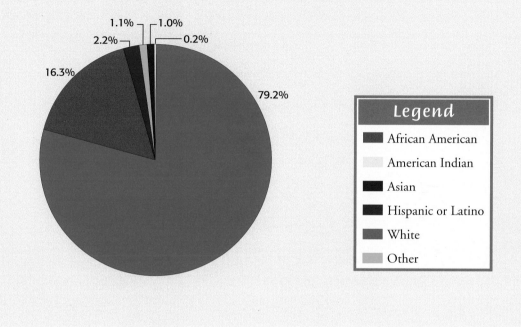

1.1%   1.0%
2.2%   0.2%
16.3%
79.2%

Legend
- African American
- American Indian
- Asian
- Hispanic or Latino
- White
- Other

Catfish is another favorite food of some Tennesseans. Many Tennesseans like their catfish fried or grilled.

Writers

Some famous writers have called Tennessee home. In 1986, Tennessean Peter Taylor won the Pulitzer Prize for *A Summons to Memphis.* The fictional novel is about a man

Lester Flatt and Earl Scruggs

Lester Flatt (left), a bluegrass guitar player and singer, was born in Duncan's Chapel, Tennessee, in 1914. Bluegrass banjo player Earl Scruggs (right) was born in Flint Hill, North Carolina, in 1924. In the mid-1940s, Flatt and Scruggs joined a band called the Blue Grass Boys. The band stayed together for about two years. Flatt and Scruggs then formed a band called the Foggy Mountain Boys. The pair produced some of the best-known bluegrass songs in history. They often played at the Grand Ole Opry. The two musicians were named to the Country Music Hall of Fame in 1985.

who leaves his home in Manhattan, New York, to visit his family and former home in Memphis, Tennessee. African American Alex Haley's book *Roots, The Saga of an American Family*, was made into a TV series. It traces his family's history through slavery.

Music

Tennessee is rich in musical heritage. This fact is reflected in the design of its state quarter. The coin features a guitar, a fiddle, and a trumpet.

Bluegrass music has its roots in the music of the Irish and Scots who settled in the mountains of Tennessee and North Carolina. The music became popular during the 1930s and 1940s.

The Grand Ole Opry is famous for its country music. It has featured country music stars such as Roy Acuff, Hank Williams Sr., Patsy Cline, and Garth Brooks.

The Grand Ole Opry attracts thousands of tourists each year.

Gospel music is popular in Tennessee. Southern slaves started African American spiritual music. Gospel music developed from the spirituals. Today, many southern church choirs sing gospel music.

Born in Mississippi, American rock music star Elvis Presley lived most of his life in Memphis. During the 1950s, Elvis combined the sound of gospel, bluegrass, and rock to make music uniquely his own. Elvis sold more than 1 billion records. Each year, thousands of visitors come to tour his former mansion, Graceland, in Memphis.

Many recording studios are located in Tennessee. Elvis recorded at Sun Studio in Memphis. The studio is known for the many famous musicians who have produced recordings there. Other studios are located in Nashville.

Tennessee has much to offer both residents and tourists. The state's diversity, economic growth, and natural beauty make it an important part of the southeastern United States.

Memphis, one of Tennessee's largest cities, is home to many of the state's most popular tourist sites and major businesses.

Recipe: Tennessee Stack Cake

This tasty treat includes apples, one of the leading fruits produced in Tennessee. Apple trees are especially common in West Tennessee.

Ingredients

4 cups (960 mL) dried sliced apples
2⅔ cups (640 mL) water
½ cup (120 mL) sugar
½ cup (120 mL) shortening
1¼ cups (300 mL) sugar
⅔ cup (160 mL) buttermilk
1 teaspoon (5 mL) baking soda
1 tablespoon (15 mL) baking powder
¼ teaspoon (1.2 mL) salt
2 teaspoons (10 mL) ground ginger
3¾ cups (895 mL) flour
8-ounce (227-gram) carton whipped cream
½ cup (120 mL) dried apple slices for decoration

Equipment

5 baking sheets
nonstick cooking spray
large saucepan
dry-ingredient measuring cups
spoon
mixing spoon
large mixing bowl
electric mixer
measuring spoons
pot holders
spatula
cooling rack
serving tray

What You Do

1. Preheat oven to 400°F (200°C). Spray baking sheets with nonstick cooking spray.

2. To make the apple filling, combine apples and water in a large saucepan. Bring to boil over medium-high heat. Reduce heat to medium-low. Simmer for 30 minutes or until apples are soft. Slightly mash the apples with spoon and stir in ½ cup (120 mL) sugar. Set aside.

3. In a large bowl, combine the shortening with 1¼ cups (300 mL) sugar and mix with electric mixer until light and fluffy. Stir in the buttermilk, baking soda, baking powder, salt, and ginger. Gradually mix in flour until dough becomes stiff.

4. Divide dough into five equal portions. On the baking sheets, pat each portion into an 8-inch (20-centimeter) circle about ¾ inch (2 centimeters) thick.

5. Bake for 10 to 12 minutes or until edges are golden brown. With spatula, place the baked circles on cooling rack and allow them to cool.

6. Stack the layers on a serving tray, spreading about ¾ cup (175 mL) of the apple filling between each layer. Cool overnight in refrigerator before serving. Top with whipped cream and dried apple slices for decoration.

Makes 6 servings

Tennessee's Flag and Seal

Tennessee's Flag

Tennessee's legislature adopted the state flag in 1905. It has a red background. A blue circle with a white border is in the center of the flag. Three white stars are in the middle of the circle. Each star stands for one of the state's regions. One thin white stripe and a blue stripe are on the flag's right side.

Tennessee's State Seal

Tennessee's state seal was adopted in 1987. The Roman numeral XVI at the top of the seal shows that Tennessee was the 16th state. The upper half of the seal features a plow, a bundle of wheat, and a cotton plant. These items stand for agriculture. A ship is at the bottom of the seal. It represents the trade of Tennessee's goods with others.

Almanac

Nicknames: Volunteer State, Big Bend State

Population: 5,689,283 (U.S. Census 2000)
Population rank: 16th

Capital: Nashville

Largest cities: Memphis, Nashville, Knoxville, Chattanooga, Clarksville

Agricultural products: Beef cattle, chickens, tobacco, cotton, dairy products, soybeans, corn, wheat

Average summer temperature: 76 degrees Fahrenheit (24 degrees Celsius)

Average winter temperature: 39 degrees Fahrenheit (4 degrees Celsius)

Average annual precipitation: 52 inches (132 centimeters)

Area: 42,146 square miles (109,158 square kilometers)
Size rank: 36th

Highest point: Clingmans Dome, 6,643 feet (2,025 meters) above sea level

Lowest point: Shelby County, 182 feet (55 meters) above sea level

Raccoon

Mockingbird

Amphibian: Tennessee cave salamander

Animal: Raccoon

Bird: Mockingbird

Flower: Iris

Gem: Tennessee River pearls

Horse: Tennessee Walking Horse

Natural resources: Coal, copper, clay, sand, stone, phosphate, zinc, barite, sulfur, lime

Types of industry: Chemicals, printing, machinery, cars, metals, electronic equipment

Songs:
"My Homeland, Tennessee,"
"My Tennessee,"
"The Tennessee Waltz,"
"Rocky Top,"
"When It's Iris Time in Tennessee"

Tree: Tulip tree

First governor: John Sevier

Statehood: June 1, 1796 (16th state)

U.S. Representatives: 9

U.S. Senators: 2

U.S. electoral votes: 11

Counties: 95

Timeline

State History

1540
Hernando de Soto explores Tennessee; at the time, Cherokee, Chickasaw, Creek, and Shawnee Indian nations are living in Tennessee.

1772
Small groups of British colonists settle in eastern Tennessee and form the Watauga Association.

1775
Daniel Boone establishes a trail through the Appalachians that was later renamed the Wilderness Road; thousands of settlers begin traveling to the Kentucky and Tennessee areas.

1796
Tennessee becomes the 16th state on June 1.

1811–1812
Earthquakes strike Tennessee, causing land in the northwestern part of the state to sink and form Reelfoot Lake.

U.S. History

1620
Pilgrims establish a colony in North America.

1775–1783
Colonists and the British fight the Revolutionary War.

1861–1865
The Union and the Confederacy fight the Civil War.

1933
The U.S. Congress forms the Tennessee Valley Authority.

1968
Martin Luther King Jr., a supporter of civil rights, is murdered in Memphis.

1993
Al Gore becomes vice president of the United States.

1914–1918
World War I is fought; the United States enters the war in 1917.

1939–1945
World War II is fought; the United States enters the war in 1941.

1964
The U.S. Congress passes the Civil Rights Act, which makes any form of discrimination illegal.

2001
On September 11, terrorists attack the World Trade Center and the Pentagon.

1929–1939
The United States experiences the Great Depression.

Words to Know

appeal (uh-PEEL)—to ask another court to review a case already decided by a lower court

basin (BAY-suhn)—a low area on the surface of the land

blues (BLOOZ)—a kind of jazz music first sung by African Americans

fossil (FOSS-uhl)—the remains or traces of an animal or plant from millions of years ago, preserved as rock

impeach (im-PEECH)—to charge an elected official for misconduct

integration (in-tuh-GRAY-shuhn)—the practice of including people of all races

missionary (MISH-uh-ner-ee)—someone who is sent by a religious group to teach that group's faith to others

secede (si-SEED)—to formally withdraw from a group or organization; the 11 Southern states seceded from the United States at the time of the Civil War.

segregation (seg-ruh-GAY-shuhn)—the practice of keeping people of one race apart from others

To Learn More

Kent, Deborah. *Tennessee.* America the Beautiful. New York: Children's Press, 2001.

Kummer, Patricia K. *Tennessee.* One Nation. Mankato, Minn.: Capstone Press, 2003.

Peck, Barbara. *Tennessee: The Volunteer State.* World Almanac Library of the States. Milwaukee: World Almanac, 2002.

Summer, L. S. *W. C. Handy: Founder of the Blues.* Journey to Freedom. Chanhassen, Minn.: Child's World, 2002.

Weatherly, Myra. *Tennesseee.* From Sea to Shining Sea. New York: Children's Press, 2001.

Internet Sites

Do you want to find out more about Tennessee?
Let FactHound, our fact-finding hound dog, do the research for you.

Here's how:
1) Visit *http://www.facthound.com*
2) Type in the Book ID number:
   0736821996
3) Click on FETCH IT.

FactHound will fetch Internet sites picked by our editors just for you!

Places to Write and Visit

Country Music Hall of Fame and Museum
222 Fifth Avenue South
Nashville, TN 37203

Grand Ole Opry
2802 Opryland Drive
Nashville, TN 37214

Great Smoky Mountains National Park
107 Park Headquarters Road
Gatlinburg, TN 37738

Office of the Secretary of State
312 Eighth Avenue North
Sixth Floor, William R. Snodgrass Tower
Nashville, TN 37243

Tennessee Department of Tourist Development
320 Sixth Avenue North
Fifth Floor, Rachel Jackson Building
Nashville, TN 37243

Tennessee Historical Society
Ground Floor, War Memorial Building
300 Capital Boulevard
Nashville, TN 37243